AM I DYING?

OR

AM I NOT?

LILY KAUR

DEDICATION

A friend of mine once said to me:

"I left you at that moment to be sad because, sometimes when you really allow yourself feel sadness, you get over it quicker."

This is for him.

And this is for you all trying and failing to pick yourselves up.

Feel the sadness till there is nothing to feel no more.

INTRODUCTION

Because at the end of the day we all have fragile hearts.

BROKEN

Trying to reach out to the very thing

that's at arm's length.

The memories of your hands running

the length of my body.

The story of your body on my fingers.

The meaning of your tongue on my skin.

I dream of you.

I ache for you.

Sometimes, I die for you.

Is that what you want?

Would that make you satisfied?

If I died for you?

CRY.

Cry for all the things you have lost.

Cry for all the moments you have lost.

Cry for the you **you** once were.

Cry for the you you are becoming.

Cry

Cry

Cry

Let yourself cry.

Then stop crying.

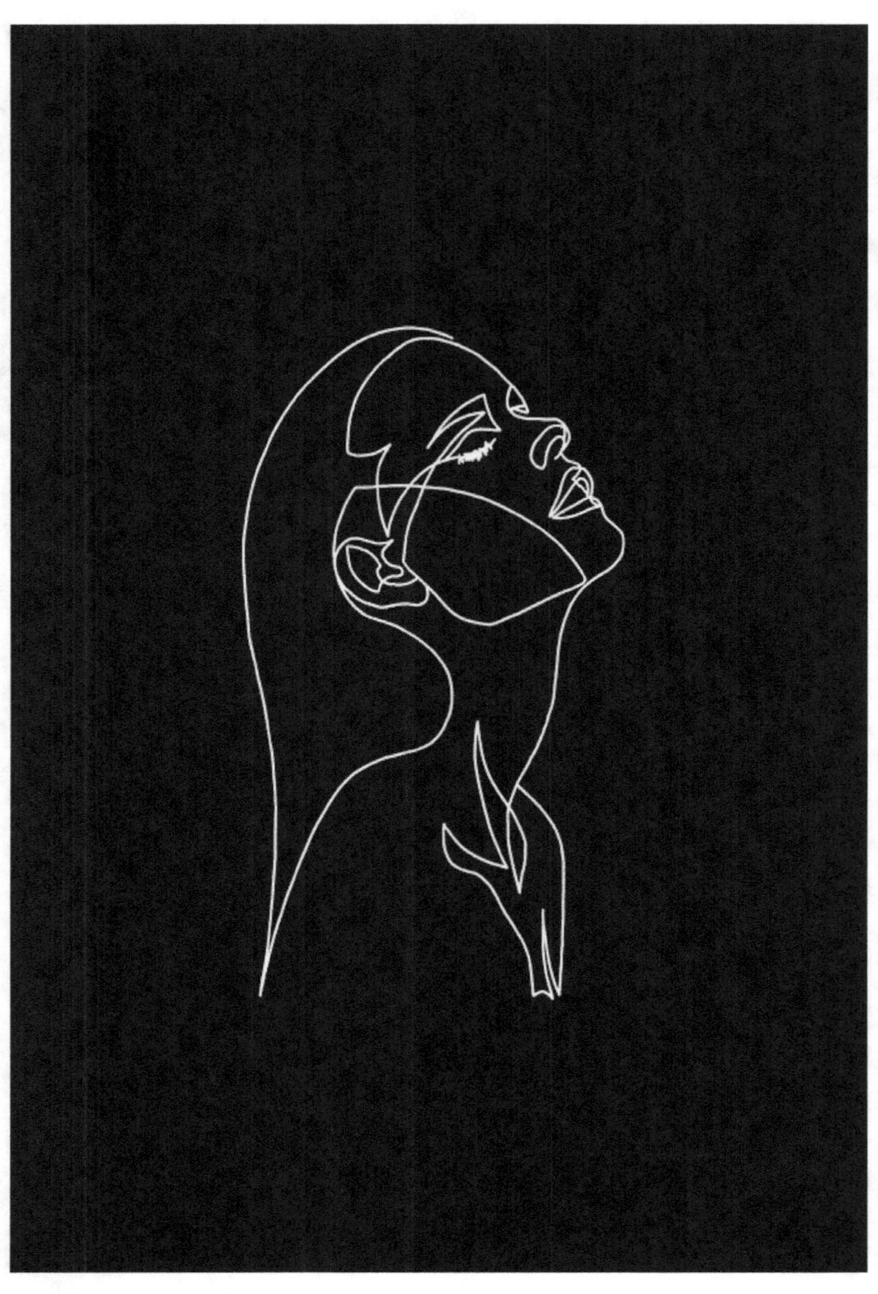

EMPTY

Who am I?

Who are we?

Sometimes I look at myself,

I see my reflection

and I'm shocked to see me

Because **I *forget***

That

I

Exist.

I know not what I want. Yet,

I long for what I want.

I yearn for the memories of what could

have been.

I am haunted by the memories of what I

have had.

I know not what I am,

I am what I know.

I know nothing.

I crave the peace. I crave the silence.

I am surrounded by the very thing that

brings the calm. Yet,

I am at war.

They say " ... though sorrow may last for

the night but joy comes in the

morning..."

But it feels like

every new day

is a blank sheet

ready to be filled

with a really long list

of bad decisions ...

...to be made

"' I thought I needed to do one more before I retired.

I still write but, you know, I'm not sending you anymore. Well at least for now.

I'm not writing for you- just so you know- I am writing for me.

I am writing because I miss you.

I am writing because the word 'miss' does not define it.

I am writing because I am frustrated and hurt and sad.''

" I am writing because even if they say letting out your emotions help, it does not.

But I write every day because even though writing does not work, it does.

It does not

I miss you.''

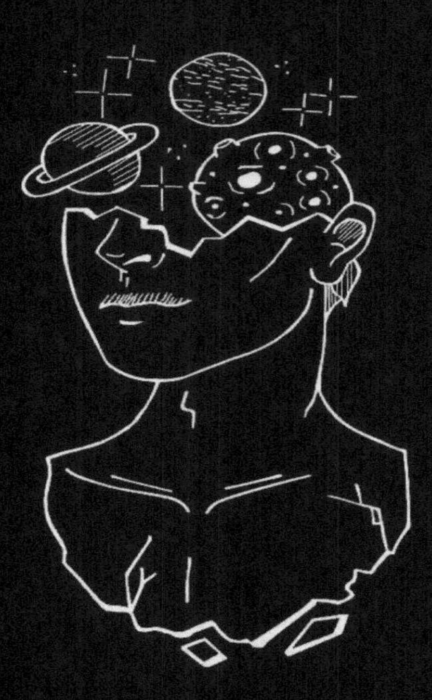

AWAKE

"Abeg. I don tire."
   - A Nigerian girl once said.

Dying makes sense sometimes.

But, I want to live.

'watched a lot of movies

read a lot of books

Everybody and everything tries to define love:

A feeling; an emotion.

A lump: an itch- the "unscratchable" itch.

A color, a smell; an aroma.

The sweet taste of freedom.

The sweet smell of flowers on a summer day.

The look of a snowflake on a beautiful winter evening...

To me?

What is love to me?

An ache I can't soothe

An itch I can't scratch

A breath lodge in my lungs I can't

release

Love is heartbreak and torment and

hurt and despair

Love is beautiful.

Don't we all love love.

Hahahahahaha.

What do you want?

Peace.

Because I have lived through the pain

I want to live

Because I have lived through the

suffering

I want to live

Because I have loved and lost and loved

I want to live

Because I have me

I want to live

And I will live.

I will so live.

And I will love.

Vicariously.

Do you still feel the sadness?

ABOUT THE AUTHOR

Lily Kaur is an accomplished master of poetry who specialized in poetics in college. She has written a lot of books and manuscripts and loves the human emotion, her favorite topics are on depression, happiness and self love. She also gives counselling whenever she can to those who need it.